Book 2

Holiday Treats

Martha Mier

D1611056

Foreword

Piano teachers are always searching for holiday solos to help their students celebrate those special days throughout the year. *Holiday Treats*, Book Two will provide teachers and students with holiday solos for an entire year, all under one cover.

The music in this collection was written especially for the elementary piano student. The solos use easy five-finger patterns with minimum shifts out of position.

I hope students will love sharing this special music with family and friends throughout the year.

Happy Holidays!

Contents

Copyright © MCMXCII by Alfred Publishing Co., Inc.
Art Direction: Ted Engelbart
Cover Design: Trish Meyer

The Pumpkin Patch Polka

Martha Mier

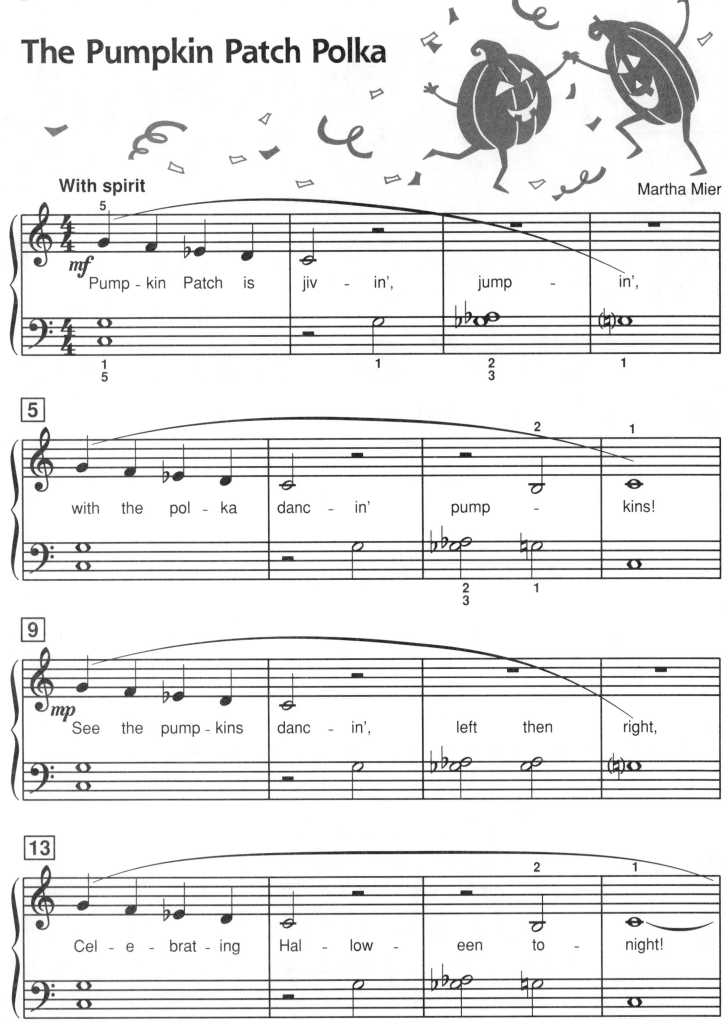

With spirit

Pump - kin Patch is jiv - in', jump - in',

5

with the pol - ka danc - in' pump - kins!

9

See the pump - kins danc - in', left then right,

13

Cel - e - brat - ing Hal - low - een to - night!

1621
(The First Thanksgiving Day)

Martha Mier

Moderately

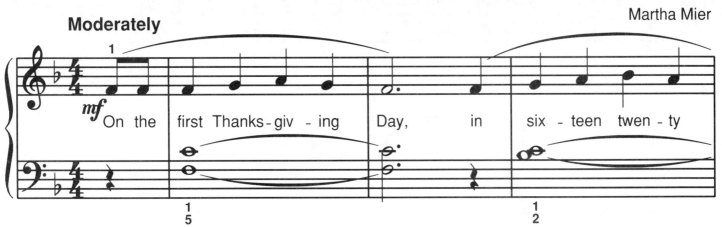

On the first Thanks-giv-ing Day, in six-teen twen-ty

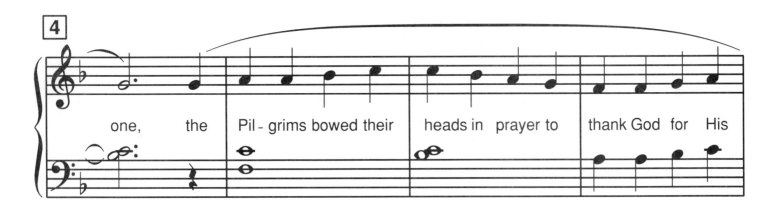

one, the Pil-grims bowed their heads in prayer to thank God for His

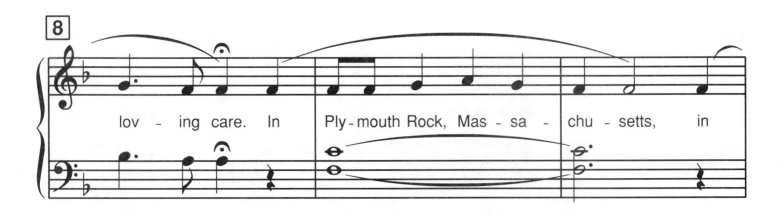

lov-ing care. In Ply-mouth Rock, Mas-sa-chu-setts, in

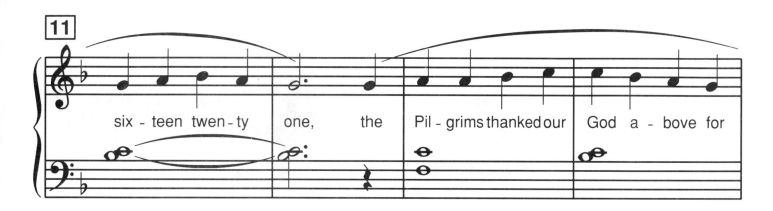

six - teen twen - ty one, the Pil - grims thanked our God a - bove for

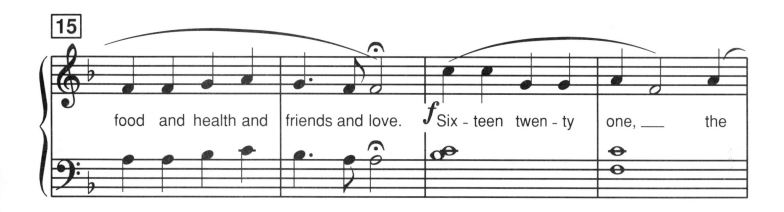

food and health and friends and love. *f* Six - teen twen - ty one, ___ the

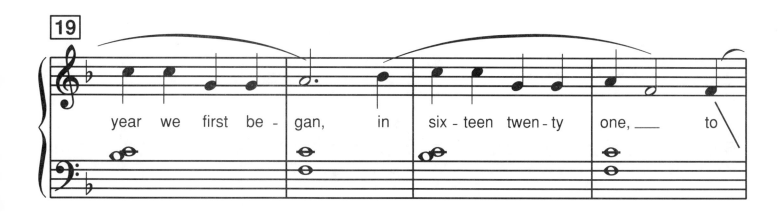

year we first be - gan, in six - teen twen - ty one, ___ to

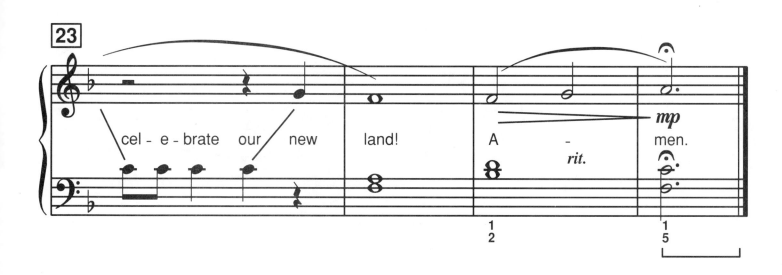

cel - e - brate our new land! A - men.

rit. *mp*

Christmas Chimes

Martha Mier

Joyfully

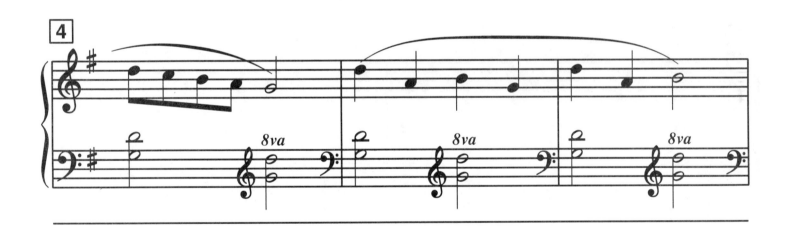

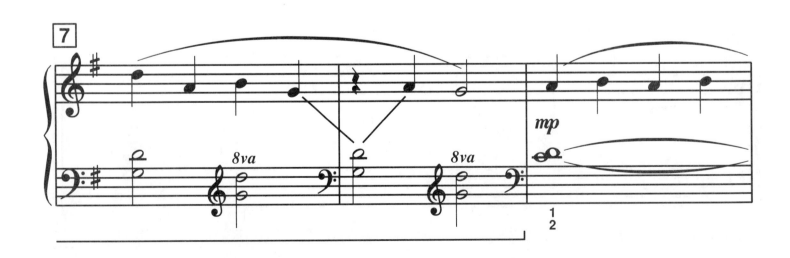

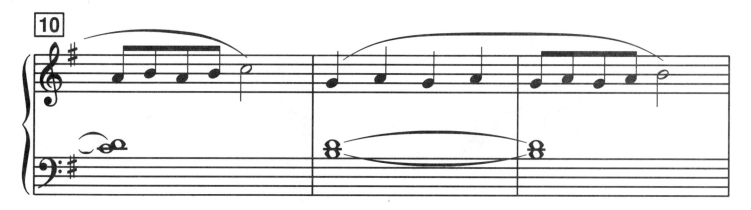

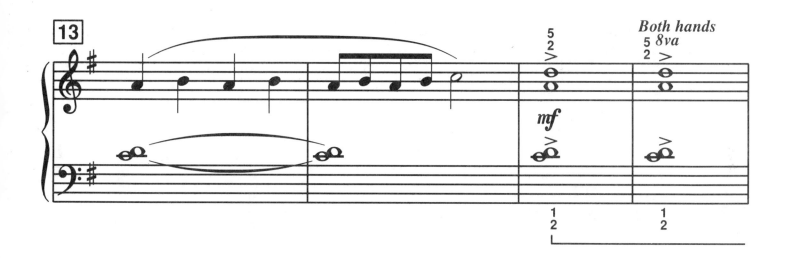

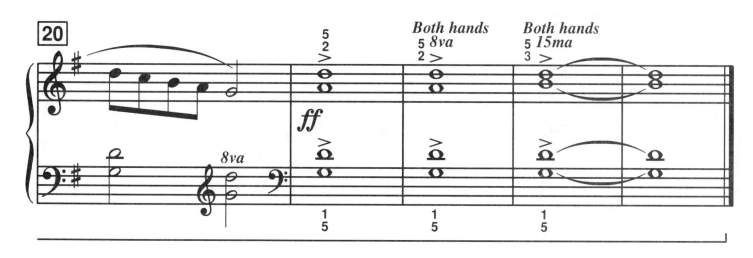

Hanukkah Dance

Martha Mier

Moderately fast

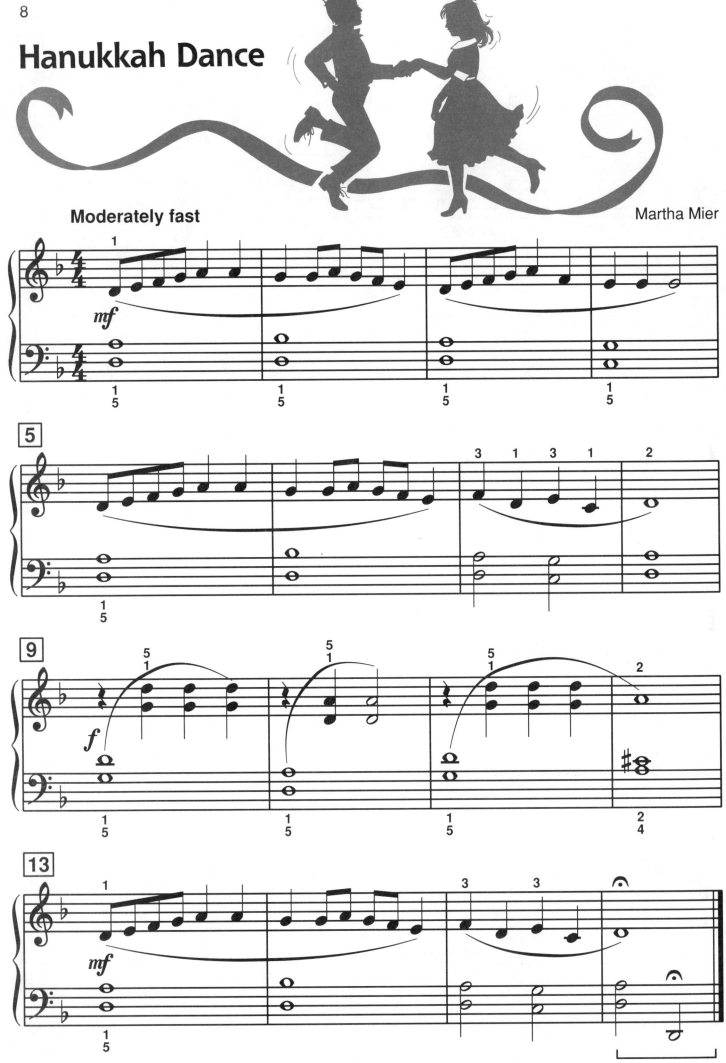

A New Year's Resolution

Martha Mier

Happily

Hap-py hap-py New Year, here's to your suc-cess; wish-ing you a grand year, filled with hap-pi-ness! Now make a New Year's res - o - lu tion and vow to keep it well: To prac - tice pian - o ev' - ry day, so that at the key-board you'll ex - cel! Hap - py New Year!

LH over 8va

Candy Hearts Waltz

Merrily

Martha Mier

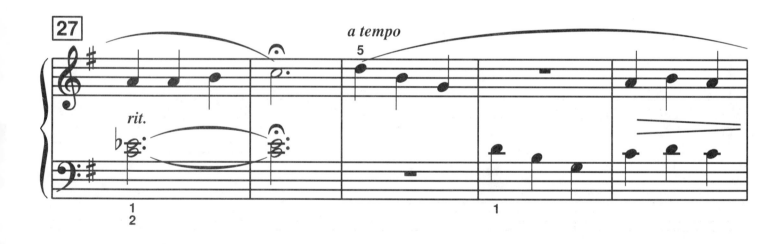

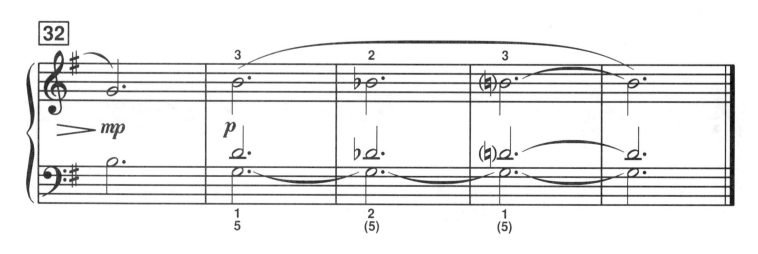

An Irish Jig

Moderately fast

Martha Mier

Play LH one octave lower throughout

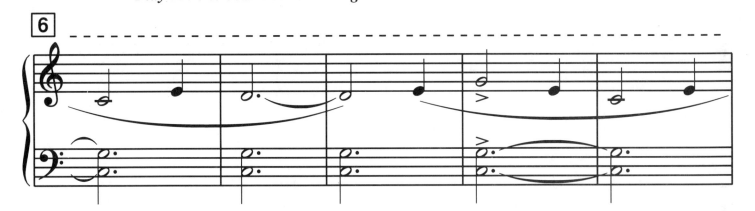

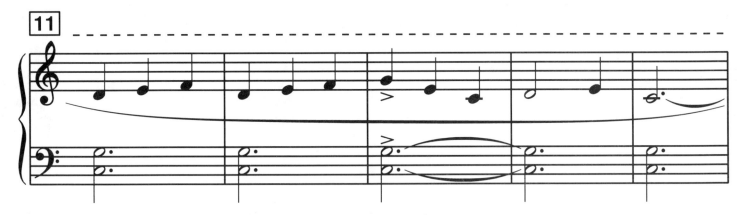

Celebration of Flags

Marching tempo

Play RH one octave higher throughout

Martha Mier

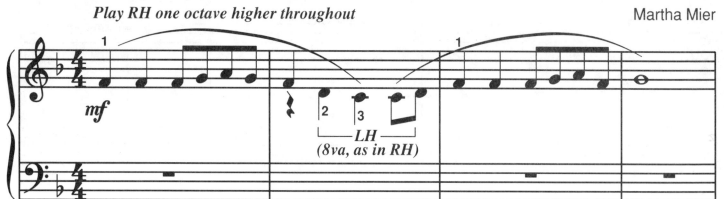

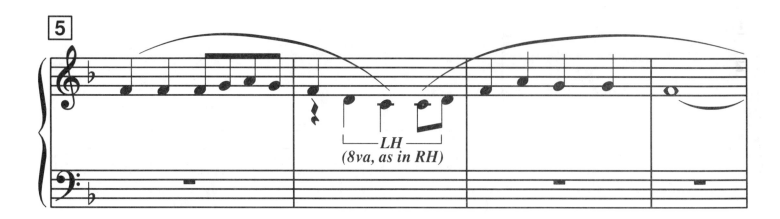

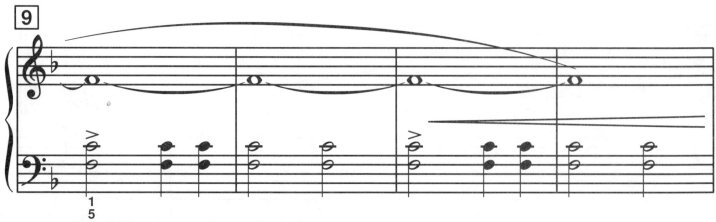

Play LH one octave lower throughout

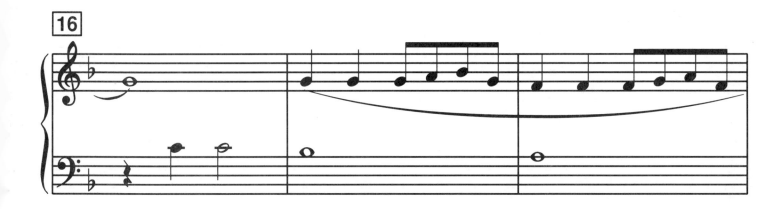

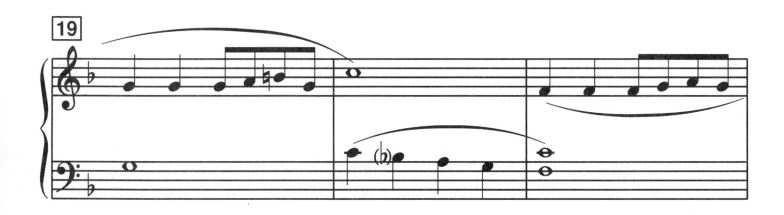

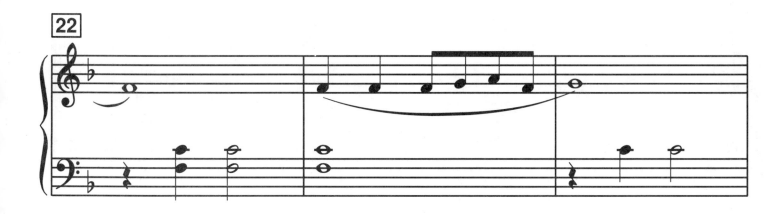

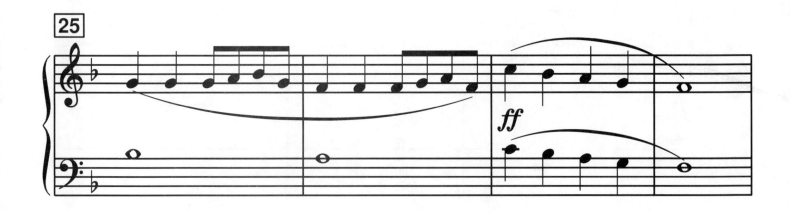

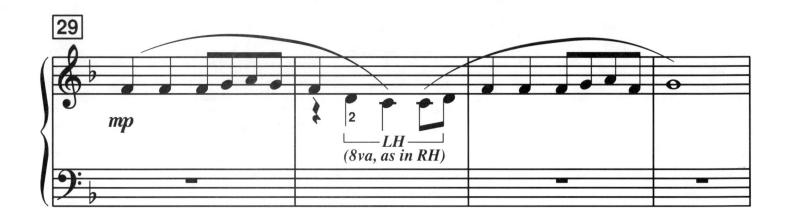

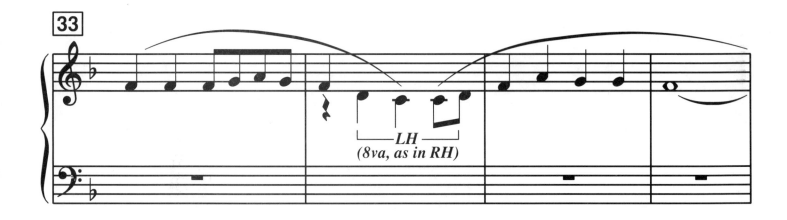

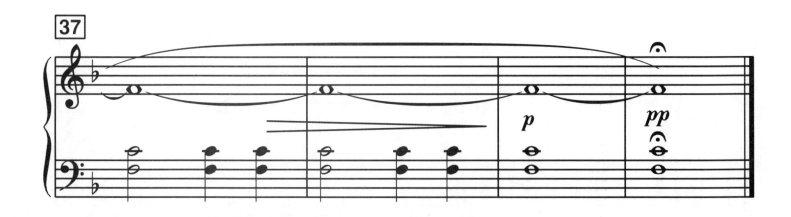